# Don't Cry,
## SCREAM

## Also By Haki R. Madhubuti

**Poetry**
*Think Black*
*Black Pride*
*Don't Cry Scream*
*We Walk the Way of the New World*
*Directionscore: Selected and New Poems*
*Book of Life*
*Earthquakes and Sunrise Mission*
*Killing Memory, Seeking Ancestors*
**Criticism**
*Dynamite Voices: Black Poets of the 1960's*
**Anthologies**
*Say That The River Turns: The Impact of*
*Gwendolyn Brooks*
*To Gwen, With Love (co-edited with Pat Brown and*
*Francis Ward)*
*Confusion By Any Other Name: Essays Exploring*
*the Negative Impact of the Blackman's Guide*
*to Understanding the Black Woman*
**Essays**
*Enemies: The Clash of Races*
*From Plan to Planet, Life Studies: The Need for*
*Black Minds and Institutions*
*A Capsuel Course in Black Poetry Writing*
*(co-authored with Gwendolyn Brooks,*
*Keorapetse Kgositsile and Dudley Randall*
*Black Men: Obsolete, Single, Dangerous? African*
*American Families in Transition*
**Records/Tapes**
*Rappin and Readin*
*Rise Vision Coming*
*(with the Afrikan Liberation Arts Ensemble)*
*Mandisa*
*(with the Afrikan Liberation Arts Ensemble)*

# DON'T CRY,
# SCREAM

by
## HAKI R. MADHUBUTI

**INTRODUCTION BY GWENDOLYN BROOKS**

THIRD WORLD PRESS
7524 So. Cottage Grove Ave.     Chicago, Illinois 60619

Third Printing, May 1992

Library of Congress catalog card number: 70:78641

ISBN: 0-88378-016-X

Third World Press
7524 S. Cottage Grove
Chicago, Illinois 60619

Some of these poems have appeared previously in
**Negro Digest, Journal of Black Poetry, Broadside
Series, Soulbook, Black Expression, Black Arts
Anthology, Fortnight, Free Lance, Nommo, The
New York Times, Ebony, Mojo and Black Cultural
Weekly.**

Cover design and illustration by
Courtney Jollif

Manufactured in the United States of America

**Dedication/myself is them/u**

first: to all blackmothers & especially mine (maxine) who will
never read this book but said to me in my early years:

> nigger, if u is going ta open
> yr/mouth **Don't Cry, Scream.**

which also means: **Don't Beg, Take.**
& second, which is really first: to realpeople, us black-
people.

gwendolyn brooks  hoyt w fuller  dudley randall  ameer
baraka  marvin x  david llorens  k william kgositsile
barbara ann teer  jewel latimore  walter bradford  james
cunningham  carolyn m rodgers  etheridge knoght  mar-
garet t g burroughs  rochelle ricks  marion graves  h rap
brown  ebon curtis ellis  regina drake  ronda davis  rand-
son c boykin  freda high  my oldman  where-ever he is
omar lama  art mcfallan  onetha  eugene perkins  ches-
er givens  jill witherspoon  sonia sanchez  pat smith
oe goncalves  s e anderson  norman jordan  ahmed
egraham alhamisi  sterling plumpp  earnestine  dondi
ee  askia muhammad toure'  jackie  pee wee  blood
arry neal  all the brothers in prison  butch  nikki giovan-
ni  mary jane  pharaoh sanders  a b spellman  francis
& val ward  ruwa chiri  lessie mims  david diop  ted
oans  gerald mcworter  stephen henderson  mari evans
sarah webster fabio  john o killens  margaret walker
catherine  bobb hamilton  margaret danner  alicia l
ohnson  betty curtis  my black students at cornell  to
hose of u whose names do not appear above  thisisu
hisisu thisisu go ahead, anyhow.
n the name of Allah, the  Beneficent, the Merciful.


As-Salaam-Alaikum,
Haki R. Madhubuti

# Contents

# A FURTHER PIONEER
## By Gwendolyn Brooks

At the hub of the new wordway is Don Lee.

Around a black audience he puts warm healing arms.

He knows that the black man today must ride full face into the whirlwind—with small regard for "correctness," with limited concern for the possibilities of "error." He knows that there are briefs even for the Big Mistake. The Big Mistake is at least a violent Change— and in the center of a violent Change are the seeds of creation.

Don Lee knows that nothing human is elegant. He is not interested in modes of writing that aspire to elegance. He is well-acquainted with "elegant" literature (what hasn't he read?) but, while certainly respecting the advantages and influence of good workmanship, he is **not** interested in supplying the needs of the English Departments at Harvard and Oxford nor the editors of Partisan Review, although he could mightily serve as fact factory for these. He speaks to blacks hungry for what they themselves refer to as **"real** poetry." These blacks find themselves and the stuff of their existence in his healthy, lithe, lusty reaches of free verse. The last thing these people crave is elegance. It is very hard to enchant, with elegant song, the ears of a fellow whose stomach is growling. He can't hear you. The more interesting noise is too loud.

Don Lee has no patience with black writers who do not direct their blackness toward black audiences. He keeps interesting facts alive in his mind. "I was born into slavery in Feb. of 1942. In the spring of that same year 110,000 persons of Japanese descent were placed in protective custody by the white people of the United States. . . . No charges had been filed against these people nor had any hearing been held. The removal of these people was on racial or ancestral grounds only. World War II, the war against racism; yet no Germans or other enemy aliens were placed in protective custody. There should have been Japanese writers directing their writings toward Japanese audiences." (Yellow writings?)

Lee's poetry is—necessarily: imperatively—capable of an awful fang and of a massive beautifully awful supersedure.

From **Malcolm Spoke/who listened?:**
animals come in all colors.
dark meat will roast as fast as whi-te meat
especially in
the unitedstatesofamerica's
new
self-cleaning ovens.

if we don't listen.


From **The Revolutionary Screw:**
brothers,
i
under/overstand
the situation: . . . . . .

From **blackmusic/a beginning:**
pharaoh sanders
had
finished
playing
&
the whi

te boy was to
go on next.

him didn't

him sd
that
his horn
was
broke.


And from **A Message All Blackpeople Can Dig:**
we'll move together
hands on weapons & families
blending into the sun,
into each/other.
we'll love,
we've always loved.
just be cool & help one/another.
go ahead.
walk a righteous direction
under the moon,
in the night
bring new meanings to
the north star,
to blackness,
to US.
discover new stars:
street-light stars that will explode into evil-eyes,
light-bulb stars visible only to the realpeople,
clean stars, african & asian stars,
black aesthetic stars that will damage the whi-te
        mind;
killer stars that will move against
the unpeople.

And always, in the center of acid, beauties that are not eaten away!

"The black writer learns from his people," says Don L. Lee. ". . . Black artists are culture stabilizers, bringing back old values, and introducing new ones."

Poetry should—"allatonce"—distil, interpret, and extend. Don Lee's poetry does.

Black poets are the authentic poets of today. Recently, one of The Critics* opined (of white poets): ". . . it's hardly surprising to find a deep longing for death as the terrible sign of their self-respect and indeed the means by which they continue to live—if not as men, at least as poets." And on: "Although death may not be the resolution of everyone's problems, it is nevertheless the one poets wait and pray for. . . ."

Can you imagine Don Lee subscribing to any of this? Black poets do not subscribe to death. When choice is possible, they choose to die only in defense of life, in defense and in honor of life.

White poetry! Never has white technique-in-general been as scintillant and various. Never has less been said. Modern corruption and precise limpness, modern narcissism, nonsense, dry winter and chains have a grotesque but granular grip on the white verse of today.

Sometimes there is a quarrel. "Can poetry be 'black'? Isn't all poetry just POETRY?" The fact that a poet is black means that his life, his history and the histories of his ancestors have been different from the histories of Chinese and Japanese poets, Eskimo poets, Indian poets,

---

*Jascha Kessler: "The Caged Sybil." **Saturday Review,** December 14, 1968.

Irish poets. The juice from tomatoes is not called merely **juice**. It is always called TOMATO juice. If you go into a restaurant desiring tomato juice you do not order the waiter to bring you "juice": you request, distinctly, TO-MATO juice. The juice from cranberries is called cranberry juice. The juice from oranges is called orange juice. The poetry from black poets is black poetry. Inside it are different nuances AND outrightnesses.

This is part of the decision of Don Lee—who is a further pioneer and a positive prophet, a prophet not afraid to be positive even though aware of a daily evolving, of his own sober and firm churning. He is a toughness. He is not a superficial toughness. He is the kind of toughness that doesn't just sass its mammy but goes right through to the bone.

## Black Poetics/for the many to come

The most significant factor about the poems/poetry you will be reading is the **idea**. The **idea** is not the manner in which a poem is conceived but the conception itself. From the **idea** we move toward development & direction (direction: the focusing of yr/idea in a positive or negative manner; depending on the poet's orientation). Poetic form is synonymous with poetic structure and is the guide used in developing yr/idea.

What u will be reading is blackpoetry. Blackpoetry is written for/to/about & around the lives/spiritactions/humanism & total existence of blackpeople. Blackpoetry in form/sound/word usage/intonation/rhythm/repetitition/direction/definition & beauty is opposed to that which is now (& yesterday) considered poetry, i.e., whi-te poetry. Blackpoetry in its purest form is diametrically opposed to white poetry. Whereas, blackpoets deal in the concrete rather than the abstract (concrete: art for people's sake; black language or Afro-american language in contrast to standard english, &c.). Blackpoetry moves to define & legitimize blackpeople's reality **(that** which is real to us). Those in power (the unpeople) control and legitimize the negroes' (the realpeople's) reality out of that which they, the unpeople, consider real. That is, to the unpeople the television programs **Julia** and **The Mod Squad** reflect their vision of what they feel the blackman **is** about or **should** be about. So, in effect, blackpoetry is out to negate the negative influences of the mass media; whether it be TV, newspapers, magazines or some whi-te boy standing on a stage saying he's a "blue eyed soul brother."

Blackpeople must move to where all confrontations with the unpeople are meaningful and constructive. That means that most, if not all, blackpoetry will be **political.** I've often come across black artists (poets, painters, actors, writers, &c.) who feel that they and their work should be apolitical; not realizing that to be apolitical is **to be** political in a negative way for blackfolks. There is **no** neutral blackart; either it **is** or it **isn't,** period. To say that one is not political is as dangerous as saying, "by any means necessary," it's an "intellectual" cop-out, & niggers are copping-out as regularly as blades of grass in a New England suburb. Being political is also why the black artist is considered dangerous by those who rule, the unpeople. The black artist by defining and legitimizing his own reality becomes a positive force in the black community (just think of the results of Le Roi Jones (Ameer Baraka) writing the lyrics for the music of James Brown). You see, **black** for the blackpoet is a way of life. And, his totalactions will reflect that blackness & he will be an example for his community rather than another contradictor.

Blackpoetry will continue to define what **is** and what **isn't.** Will tell what is **to be** & how to **be** it (or bes it). Blackpoetry **is** and will continue to be an important factor in culture building. I believe Robert Hayden had culture building in mind when he wrote these lines in an early poem:

> It is time to call the children
> Into the evening quiet of the living-room
> And teach them the legends of their blood.

Blackpoetry is excellence & truth and will continue to seek such. Blackpoetry will move to expose & wipe-out that which is not necessary for our existence as a people. **As a people** is the only way we can endure and black-nation building must accelerate at top speed. Black-poetry is Ornette Coleman teaching violin & the Supremes being black again. Blackpoetry is like a razor; it's sharp & will cut deep, not out to wound but to kill the inactive blackmind. Like, my oldman used to pickup numbers and he seldom got caught & I'm faster than him; this is a fight with well defined borders & I know the side I'm ON. See u. Go head, now.

As-Salaam Alaikum
don l. lee

To the keen clamour of the Negro from Africa to the
    Americas
It is the sign of the dawn
The sign of brotherhood which comes to nourish
    the dreams of men.

        From the poem **Listen Comrades** by
        David Diop

In a land where the way of life is understood
Race-horses are led back to serve the field;
In a land where the way of life is not understood
War-horses are bred on the autumn yield.

There is no need to run outside
For better seeing,
Nor to peer from a window. Rather abide
At the center of your being;
For the more you leave it, the less you learn.
Search your heart and see
If he is wise who takes each turn:
The way to do is to be.

From **The Way of Life** According to
Lao Tzu

The black artist. The black man. The holy holy black man. The man you seek. The climber the striver. The maker of peace. The lover. The warrior. We are they whom you seek. Look in. Find yr self. Find the being, the speaker. The voice, the black dust hover in your soft eyeclosings. Is you. Is the creator. Is nothing. Plus or minus, you vehicle! We are presenting. Your various selves. We are presenting, from God, a tone, your own. Go on. Now.

From the FOREWORD to **Black Fire,**
Le Roi Jones (Ameer Baraka)

## Gwendolyn Brooks

she doesn't wear
costume jewelry
& she knew that walt disney
was/is making a fortune off
false-eyelashes and that time magazine is the
authority on the knee/grow.
her makeup is total-real.


a negro english instructor called her:
    "a fine negro poet."
a whi-te critic said:
    "she's a credit to the negro race."
somebody else called her:
    "a pure negro writer."
johnnie mae, who's a senior in high school said:
    "she & langston are the only negro poets we've
    read in school and i understand her."
pee wee used to carry one of her poems around in his
    back pocket;
    the one about being cool. that was befo pee wee
    was cooled by a cop's warning shot.


into the sixties
a word was born . . . . . . . . BLACK
& with black came poets
& from the poet's ball points came:
black doubleblack purpleblack blueblack beenblack was
black daybeforeyesterday blackerthan ultrablack super
black blackblack yellowblack niggerblack blackwhi-te-
    man
blackerthanyoueverbes ¼ black unblack coldblack clear

black my momma's blackerthanyourmomma pimpleblack
    fall
black so black we can't even see you black on black in
black by black technically black mantanblack winter
black coolblack 360degreesblack coalblack midnight
black black when it's convenient rustyblack moonblack
black starblack summerblack electronblack spaceman
black shoeshineblack jimshoeblack underwearblack ugly
black auntjimammablack, uncleben'srice black
    williebest
black blackisbeautifulblack i justdiscoveredblack negro
black unsubstanceblack.

and everywhere the
lady "negro poet"
appeared the poets were there.
they listened & questioned
& went home feeling uncomfortable/unsound & so-
    untogether
they read/re-read/wrote & re-wrote
& came back the next time to tell the
lady "negro poet"
how beautiful she was/is & how she had helped them
& she came back with:
    how necessary they were and how they've helped her.
the poets walked & as space filled the vacuum between
    them & the
lady "negro poet"
u could hear one of the blackpoets say:
    "bro, they been callin that sister by the wrong name."

**But He Was Cool**
## or: he even stopped for green lights

super-cool
ultrablack
a tan/purple
had a beautiful shade.


he had a double-natural
that wd put the sisters to shame.
his dashikis were tailor made
& his beads were imported sea shells
    (from some blk/country i never heard of)
he was triple-hip.


his tikis were hand carved
out of ivory
& came express from the motherland.
he would greet u in swahili
& say good-by in yoruba.
wooooooooooooo-jim he bes so cool & ill tel li gent
          cool-cool is so cool he was un-cooled by
              other niggers' cool
          cool-cool ultracool was bop-cool/ice box
              cool so cool cold cool
          his wine didn't have to be cooled, him was
              air conditioned cool
          cool-cool/real cool made me cool—now
              ain't that cool
          cool-cool so cool him nick-named refrig-
              erator.


cool-cool so cool
he didn't know,

after detroit, newark, chicago &c.,
we had to hip
        cool-cool/ super-cool/ real cool
   that
to be black
is
to be
very-hot.

## communication in whi-te

dee dee dee dee dee wee weee eeeeee wee we
      deweeeeeeee ee ee ee nig
nig nig nig niggggggggggggggggggg cleek cleek cleek
      cleeeeee cleekcleek
rip rip rip rip rip/rip/rip/rip/rip/ripripripripripripripri
      pi pi pi pi pip
bom bom bom bom bom/bom/bom/bombombombom
      bombbombbombbombbombbomb
deathtocleekdeathtocleekdeath tocleekdeathtocleek
      deathtocleekdeathtodeathto
allllllllllllallllllllllll alllllllllllll deathtoalllllllll alllllllllll
      alllllllleeeeeeee
te te te te te te  te/te/te/te/te/te/tetetetetetetetetete
      tetetetetetetete:
the paris peace talks, 1968.

**DON'T CRY, SCREAM**
**(for John Coltrane/ from a black poet/**
**in a basement apt. crying dry tears**
**of "you ain't gone.")**

into the sixties
a trane
came/ out of the
fifties with a
golden boxcar
riding the rails
of novation.
       blowing
       a-melodics
       screeching,
       screaming,
       blasting—
              driving some away,
              (those paper readers who thought
              manhood was something innate)

              bring others in,
              (the few who didn't believe that the
              world existed around established whi
              teness & leonard bernstein)
music that ached.
murdered our minds (we reborn)
born into a neoteric aberration.
& suddenly
you envy the
BLIND man—
you know that he will
hear what you'll never
see.

your music is like
my head—nappy black/
a good nasty feel with
tangled songs of:
    we-eeeeeeeeeee          sing
    WE-EEEeeeeeeeeee    loud &
    WE-EEEEEEE EEEEEEEEEE high
                                  with
                                  feeling

a people playing
the sound of me when
i combed it. combed at
it.

i cried for billy holiday.
the blues. we ain't blue
the blues exhibited illusions of manhood.
destroyed by you. Ascension into:

    scream-eeeeeeeeeeeeee-ing       sing
    SCREAM-EEEeeeeeeeeeee-ing   loud &
    SCREAM-EEEEEEEEEEE EEE-ing  long with
                                  feeling

we ain't blue, we are black.
we ain't blue, we are black.
                (all the blues did was
                make me cry)
soultrane gone on a trip
he left man images
he was a life-style of
man-makers & annihilator
of attache case carriers.

Trane done went.
(got his hat & left me one)

naw brother,
i didn't cry,
i just—

Scream-eeeeeeeeeeeee e-ed       sing loud
SCREAM-EEEEEEEEEEE EEEEEEE-ED    & high with
  we-eeeeeeeeeee eeeeeeeeee ee    feeling
  WE-EEEEEEeeeeeeeee EEEEEEEE    letting
  WE-EEEEEEEEEEEEEEEEEEEEEEEE    yr/voice
  WHERE YOU DONE GONE, BROTHER? break

it hurts, grown babies
dying. born. done caught me
a trane. steel wheels broken
by popsicle sticks. i went out
& tried to buy a nickle bag
with my standard oil card.

blonds had more fun—
with snagga-tooth niggers
who saved pennies & pop bottles for week-ends
to play negro & other filthy inventions.
be-bop-en to james brown's
**cold sweat**—these niggers didn't sweat,
they perspired. & the blond's dye came out,
 ran. she did too, with his pennies, pop bottles
& his mind. tune in next week same time same station
or anti-self in one lesson.

30

to the negro cow-sissies
who did tchaikovsky &
the beatles & live in
split-level homes & had
split-level minds & babies.
who committed the act of
love with their clothes on.

   (who hid in the bathroom to read
   jet mag., who didn't read the chicago
   defender because of the misspelled
   words & had shelves of books by
   europeans on display. untouched. who
   hid their little richard & lightnin'
   slim records & asked: "John who?"


   instant hate.)
they didn't know any better,
brother, they were too busy getting
into debt, expressing humanity &
taking off color.


  SCREAMMMM/we-eeeee/screech/teee improvise
  aheeeeeeee/screeeeeee/theeee/ee  with
  ahHHHHHHHHH/WEEEEEEEE/scrEEE feeling
   EEEE
  we-eeeeeeWE-EEEEEEEEWE-EE- EEEEE
the ofays heard you &
were wiped out. spaced.
one clown asked me during,
**my favorite things,** if
you were practicing.
i fired on the muthafucka & said,
"i'm practicing."

naw brother,
i didn't cry.
i got high off my thoughts—
they kept coming back,
back to destroy me.

& that BLIND man
i don't envy him anymore
i can see his hear
& hear his heard through my pores.
i can see my me. it was truth you gave,
like a daily shit
it had to come.

        can you scream—brother?    very
        can you scream—brother?    soft

i hear you.
i hear you.

and the Gods will too.

## Assassination

it was wild.

the

bullet hit high.

(the throat-neck)

& from everywhere:

the motel, from under bushes and cars,
from around corners and across streets,
out of the garbage cans and from rat holes
in the earth

they came running.

with

guns

drawn

they came running

toward the King—

all of them

fast and sure—

as if

the King

was going to fire back.

they came running,

fast and sure,

in the

wrong

direction.

**Malcolm Spoke/ who listened?**
**(this poem is for my consciousness too)**

    he didn't say
    wear yr/blackness in
    outer garments
    & blk/slogans fr/the top 10.

    he was fr a long
    line of super-cools,
        doo-rag lovers &
        revolutionary pimps.
    u are playing that
    high-yellow game in blackface
    minus the straighthair.
    now
    it's nappy-black
    & air conditioned volkswagens
    with undercover whi
    te girls who studied faulkner at
    smith
    & are authorities on "militant"
    knee/grows
    selling u at jew town rates:
        niggers with wornout tongues
        three for a quarter/ or will consider a trade

    the double-breasted hipster
    has been replaced with a
    dashiki wearing rip-off
    who went to city college
    majoring in physical education.

    animals come in all colors.
    dark meat will roast as fast as whi-te meat

especially in
the unitedstatesofamerica's
new
self-cleaning ovens.

if we don't listen.


## From A Black Perspective

wallace for president
his momma for vice-president

was scribbled
on the men's room wall
on
over
the toilet

where
it's
supposed to be.

## Blackrunners/blackmen
### or run into blackness

(for brothers tommie smith & john carlos—
super-sprinters—but  most  of  all  blackmen)

u beat them
brothers;
at their own game.
      (outran  the  world-runners)
whi-te boys
& others
had a dust-meal.

u beat them.
now
in this time in space
the rule-makers
are  also
the  vanquished.

anyhow/way
we can't eat gold medals
& sportsmanship is racism
in three syllables.

u beat them brothers
and u/we
will beat them again.
they
just don't know
that
u've/got friends
&
we know how to
fight dirty.

**a poem to complement other poems**

change.

life if u were a match i wd light u into something beauti-
ful. change.

change.

for the better into a realreal together thing. change, from
a make believe

nothing on corn meal and water. change.

change. from the last drop to the first, maxwellhouse
did. change.

change was a programmer for IBM, thought him was a
brown computor. change.

colored is something written on southern out-
houses. change.

grayhound did, i mean they got rest rooms on buses.
change.

change.

change nigger.

saw a nigger hippy, him wanted to be different. changed.

saw a nigger liberal, him wanted to be different.
changed.

saw a nigger conservative, him wanted to be different.
changed.

niggers don't u know that niggers are different. change.

a doublechange. nigger wanted a double zero in front of
his name; a license to kill,

niggers are licensed to be killed. change. a negro: some-
thing pigs eat.

change. i say change into a realblack righteous aim. like
i don't play

saxophone but that doesn't mean i don't dig 'trane.'
change.

change.
hear u coming but yr/steps are too loud. change. even a
	lamp post changes nigger.
change, stop being an instant yes machine. change.
niggers don't change they just grow. that's a change;
	bigger & better niggers.
change, into a necessary blackself.
change, like a gas meter gets higher.
change, like a blues song talking about a righteous to-
	morrow.
change, like a tax bill getting higher.
change, like a good sister getting better.
change, like knowing wood will burn. change.
know the realenemy.
change,
change nigger: standing on the corner, thought him was
			cool. him still
			standing there. it's winter time, him cool.
change,
know the realenemy.
change: him wanted to be a TV star. him is. ten o'clock
			news.
		wanted, wanted. nigger stole some lemon & lime
			popsicles,
		thought them were diamonds.
change nigger change.
know the realenemy.
change: is u is or is u aint. change. now now change. for
			the better change.
		read a change. live a change. read a blackpoem.
			change. be the realpeople.
		change. blackpoems
will change:

know the realenemy. change. know the realenemy. change
    yr/enemy change know the real
change know the realenemy change, change, know the
    realenemy, the realenemy, the real
realenemy change your the enemies/ change your change
    your change your enemy change
your enemy. know the realenemy, the world's enemy.
    know them know them know them the
realenemy  change your enemy  change your change
    change change your enemy change change
change change your change change change.
your
mind nigger.


## Hero

> (a poem for brig. general frederic davison,
> if he can dig it)

little willie
a hero in
the american tradition.
a blk/hero.
he
received the:
> bronze star: which read "meritorious action,"
> > (his momma had to look the word up)
>
> good conduct medal,
> combat infantry badge,
> purple heart,
> national defense service medal,
> vietnam campaign ribbon,
> & some others i can't even spell.

little willie
a hero in
the american tradition.
a blk/hero.
he
received his medals

p
o
s
t
h
u
m
o
u
s
l
y
.
.
.

## History of The Poet as a Whore
    (to all negro poets who deal in whi-te paronomasia)

yeats in brown-tone
ultrablack with a whi-te tan,
had a dangerous notion that
he/she
wd be famous yesterday.
a paper prostitute
with ink stained contraceptions.
still,
acute fear of colored pregnancy
forces poet to be poet
& not "negro poet" (supposedly a synonym for blk/poet)
whose poem-poems are conceived in
nine month intervals
with a
rarity of miscarriages tho most are
premature.
whereas R.A.M.* becomes
royal academy of music
& another poet's poem
aid in
mental genocide of blackpeople
while
he/she switches down the
street with
his/her ass wide-open bleeding
whi-te blood.

———

*Revolutionary Action Movement

**a poem for negro intellectuals**
                        (if there bes such a thing)
                &
                blackwoman be ahead
                moved
                un-noticed
                throughout the
                world
                a people deathliving
                in
                abstract realities
                hoping/looking
                for
                blk/man-actions
                from
                action-livers.

                &
                blackmen,
                action-givers to the
                world
                unknown to
                yr/own

                will
                unlike yes
                terday
                again
                be born into
                a
                blk/self.

                u
                will move

as swift as
black d.c. sevens
or as
sharprazors fr/blk/hands
swinging
among mid-night stars
where
everything is
in
place
as it was
yes
   terday &
yes
terday &
yes
it will not be so tomorrow,
if we do.

## Nigerian Unity/ or little niggers killing little niggers
### (for brothers Christopher Okigbo & Wole Soyinka)

suppose those
who made
wars
had to fight them?

it's called blackgold.
& you,
my brothers/former warriors
who use to own the nights
that
knew no boarders
have acquired strings on yr/minds
& have knowingly sold yr/our/mothers.
there are no more tears.
tears will not stop bullets.
the dead don't cry,
the dead just grow; good crop this year,
wouldn't u say.

it's called blackgold
& u fight blindly,
swinging at yr/own mid-nights,
at yr/own children of tomorrow.

come   one   come   two
against the middle is
a double feature starring the man from u.n.c.l.e.
with a nigger on his back
who played ping-pong with christ
and won.

little niggers
killing

little niggers: ontime/intime/outoftime
          theirtime/otherpeople'stime as
          niggers killed niggers everytime.

suppose those
who made
wars
had to fight them?

blackgold is not
the newnigger:
with a british accent
called me 'old chap' one day,
i rubbed his skin
it didn't come off. even him surprised.

him
another pipe-smoking faggot
who lost his balls in
a double-breasted suit
walking thru a nadinola commercial
with a degree in european history.
little nigger
choked himself with a hippy's tie
his momma didn't even know him/
          she thought he was a TWA flashback or
          something out of a polka-dot machine.
he
cursed at her in perfect english
called her:
Mother-Dear.

WANTED      WANTED
     black warriors to go south
     to fight in Africa's mississippi.
go south young man.

everybody missed that train,
except one sister.
she wanted to fight the realenemy
but
she was "uneducated,"
wore the long-dress
talked the native tongue
& had a monopoly on blackbeauty.
when we met—she smiled & said: "i'm the true gold,
$\qquad$ i'm the real-gold."

suppose those
who made
wars
had to fight them?

the real blackgold
was there before the drill,
before the dirty-eyed,
before the fence-builders,
before the wells,
before the british accent,
before christ,
before air condition,
before the cannon,
the real blackgold: was momma & sister; **is** momma &
    sister.
was there before the "educated,"
before the pig-eaters,
before the cross-wearers,
before the pope,
before the nigger-warriors.
the real blackgold
was the first warrior.

go south young man.

little niggers
killing
little niggers.
the weak against the weak.
the ugly against the ugly.
the powerless against the powerless.
the realpeople becoming unpeople
& brothers we have more in common
than pigmentation & stupidity.
that same old two-for-one
was played on 47th & ellis—
invented on 125 & lenox
and now is double-dealing from
the mangrove swamps to the savannah grassland;
2 niggers for the price of nothing.

newnigger
lost his way
a whi-te girl gave him direction
him still lost
she sd whi-te/he thought bite
been eating everything in sight
including himself.

suppose those
who made
wars
had to fight them?

the lone ranger got a new tonto
he's 'brown' with a Ph.D. in
psy-chol-o-gy
& still walks around with
holes
in his brain.
losthismind.

saw him the other day
with his head across some railroad tracks—
tryin to get an untan.
will the real jesus christ
**please** stand up
and take a bow;
u got niggers tryin to be trains.

trained well.
european-african took a
**double**
at oxford.
wears ban-lon underwear & whi-te socks,
has finally got the killer's eye,
join the deathbringers club
& don't want more than two children.

the real blackgold
will be crippled,
raped,
and killed
in
that
order.

i will miss
the joy
of calling her
sister

go south young man.

suppose those
who made
wars
had to fight **you.**

## blackmusic/a beginning

> pharaoh sanders
> had
> finished
> playing
> &
> the whi-
> te boy was to
> go on next.
>
> him didn't
>
> him sd
> that
> his horn
> was
> broke.
>
> they sat
> there
> dressed in
> african garb
> & dark sun glasses
> listening to the brothers
> play.    (taking notes)
> we
> didn't realize
> who they
> were un
> til their
> next recording
> had been
> released: the beach boys play soulmusic.

real sorry about
the supremes
being dead,
heard some whi
te girls
the other day—
all wigged-down
with a mean tan—
soundin just like them,
singin
rodgers & hart
& some country & western.

**Black Sketches**
1

i
was five
when
mom & dad got married
& i
didn't realize that
i
was illegitimate
until i started
school.


2

i was at
the airport
& had
to use the
men's room
real bad
& didn't have a
dime.


3

sombody
made a
mistake (they said)
&
sent the
peace corps to
europe.

4

went to cash
my
1968 tax refund
&
the check bounced;
insufficient funds.


5

i
read the
newspapers today
&
thought that
everything
was
all right.


6

nat turner
returned
&
killed
william styron
&
his momma too.

52

7

ed brooke
sat at his
desk
crying & slashing
his wrist
because somebody
called him
black.


8

general westmoreland
was transferred
to the
westside of chicago
&
he lost
there too.


9

in 1959
my mom
was dead at the
age of
35
& nobody thought it unusual;
not even
me.

10

in 1963
i
became black
& everyone thought it unusual;
even me.

11

the american dream:
          nigger bible in
          every hotel;
          iceberg slim (pimp) getting
          next to julia;
          & roy wilkins on
          the mod squad.

**blackwoman:**

> will define herself. naturally. will
> talk/walk/live /& love her images. her
> beauty will be. the only way to be is
> to be. blackman take her. u don't need
> music to move; yr/movement toward her
> is music. & she'll do more than dance.

## BLACKWOMAN

blackwoman:
is an
in and out
rightsideup
action-image
of her man. . . . . . . . .
in other
(blacker) words;
she's together,
**if**
**he**
**bes.**

## The Third World Bond

(for my sisters & their sisters)

they were
blk/revolutionist.
& they often talked
of the third world
& especially of the power
of
china.
(quoting mao every 3rd word)
they were
revolutionist
& the blk/sisters knew it
& looked,
& wondered
while the brothers/
the revolutionists,
made bonds
with the
3rd world
thru
chinese women.
the sisters waited.
(& wondered when the revolution would start)

## The Revolutionary Screw
(for my blacksisters)

brothers,
i
under/overstand
the situation:

i mean—
    u bes hitten the man hard
    all day long.
a stone revolutionary, "a full time revolutionary."
    tellen the man how bad u is
    & what u goin ta do
    & how u goin ta do it.

it must be a bitch
to be able to do all that
talken. (& not one irregular breath fr/yr/mouth)
being so
foreful & all
to the man's face (the courage)
& u not even cracken a smile (realman).

i know,
the sisters just don't
understand the
pressure u is under.

&
when u ask for a piece
of leg/
it's not for yr/self
but for
yr/people————it keeps u going
& anyway u is a revolutionary

& she wd be doin
a revolutionary thing.

that sister dug it
from the beginning,
had an early-eye.
i mean
she really had it together
when she said:
            go fuck yr/self nigger.

now
that was
revolutionary.

## Reflections on a Lost Love

> (for my brothers who think they are lovers
> and my sisters who are the real-lovers)

back in chi/
all the blackwomen
are fine,
super fine.
even the ones who:
     dee bob/de bop/ she-shoo-bop
     bop de-bop/ dee dee bop/ dee-she dee-she-bop
     we--We eeeeeeeeeeeeeee/ WEEEEEEE EEEEEEEE
they so fine/
that
when i slide up
to one & say:  take it off          sing
               take it off          slow
                    take it all off     with feeling

& she would say: "if i doos,
             does us think u can groove dad——dy"
& i wd say: "can chitlins smell,
        is toejam black,
        can a poet, poet,
        can a musician, music?"

        weeeee/weeeeeee/ de-bop-a-dee-bop
        whooo-bop/dee-bop a-she-bop
as she smiled
& unbuttoned that top button
i sd:  take it off        sing
          take it off        slow
              take it all off     with feeling

fiirst the skirt,
then the blouse
& next her wig (looked like she made it herself)
next the shoes & then
the eyelashes and jewelry
&
    dee-bop/ bop-a-ree-bop/ WOW
the slip
& next the bra (they weren't big, but that didn't scare me)
cause i was grooven now: dee/ dee-bop-a-she-bop/
    weeeeeEEEEEEEEEE
as she moved to the most important part,
i got up & started to groove myself but my eyes stopped
    me.
first
her stockens down those shapely legs—
followed by black bikini panties, that just slid down
and
i just stood—
& looked with utter amazement as she said:   in a deep
        "hi baby—my name is   man-like
        joe sam."       voice

## A Poem Looking for a Reader
### (to be read with a love consciousness)

black is not
all inclusive,
there are other colors.
color her warm and womanly,
color her feeling and life,
color her a gibran poem & 4 women of simone.
children will give her color
paint her the color of her
man.

most of all color her
love
a remembrance of life
a truereflection
that we
will
move    u will move with
i want
u
a fifty minute call to blackwomanworld:
        hi baby,
        how u doin?
need u.
listening to
young-holt's, **please sunrise, please.**

to give    i'll give
most personal.
what about the other
scenes: children playing in vacant lots,
        or like the first time u knowingly kissed a girl,
        was it joy or just beautifully beautiful.

i
remember at 13
reading chester himes'
**cast the first stone** and
the eyes of momma when she caught me: read on, son.

how will u come:
    like a soulful strut in a two-piece beige o-rig'i-nal,
    or afro-down with a beat in yr/walk?
how will love come:
    painless and deep like a razor cut
    or like some cheap 75c movie;
    i think not.

will she be the woman
other men will want
or
will her beauty be
accented with my name on it?

she will come as she would
want her man to come.
she'll come,
she'll come.
i
never wrote a love letter
but
that doesn't mean
i
don't love.

## A Message All Blackpeople Can Dig
### ( & a few negroes too)

we are going to do it.
US: blackpeople, beautiful people; the sons and daugh-
    ters of beautiful people.
bring it back to
US: the unimpossibility.
now is
the time, the test
while there is something to save (other than our lives).

we'll move together
hands on weapons & families
blending into the sun,
into each/other.
we'll love,
we've always loved.
just be cool & help one/another.
go ahead.
walk a righteous direction
under the moon,
in the night
bring new meanings to
the north star,
the blackness,
to US.

discover new stars:
street-light stars that will explode into evil-eyes,
light-bulb stars visible only to the realpeople,
clean stars, african & asian stars,
black aesthetic stars that will damage the whi-temind;

killer stars that will move against
the unpeople.

came
brothers/fathers/sisters /mothers/sons /daughters
dance as one
walk slow & hip.
hip to what life is
and can be.
& remember we are not hippies,
WE WERE BORN HIP.
walk on. smile a little
yeah, that's it beautiful people
move on in,   take   over.   take over, take over take/over
          takeovertakeovertakeover
     takeovertakeover   overtakeovertakeovertake over/
          take over take, over take,
     over  take, over   take.
blackpeople
are moving, moving to return
     this earth into the hands of

human beings.